Cultivating Your Light Body
A Handbook

Living in the Center of the Circle of the Heart

Including
Meditations to Reconnect and Energize Your Light Body

Dr. Patrick MacManaway MB.ChB.

Cultivating Your Light Body, A Handbook
Author: Dr. Patrick MacManaway
Design and Graphic Illustrations: David Brizendine
Paintings: Alya MacManaway
Published by the Simply Good Company
© 2011 Patrick MacManaway
ISBN: 978-0-9833953-3-1
www.SimplyGoodCo.com
www.PatrickMacManaway.com

in the spirit of loving service...

"this knowledge comes with the responsibility of sharing it..."

Hello, and welcome to this simple little study of the human light body - designed to introduce you to the invisible part of yourself - the part of yourself that holds pattern and form for the physical framework - the part of yourself that holds and defines the quality of your spirit, the tone of your feelings, the content and quality of your thoughts.

The part of yourself perhaps that is most truly yourself - the part of yourself perhaps that is the source of your power and presence.

When we look around ourselves at the very many things in our world, we see, at first appearance, a rich and sometimes overwhelming diversity of complex and complicated forms and shapes, large and small, moving and still, animal mineral and vegetable.

We spend much of our time fascinated and preoccupied by the ways in which things appear different and unique one to another, and wonder, with so many degrees of variation and otherness, where and how we fit and belong in such complication ourselves - what the nature and meaning of humanness might be.

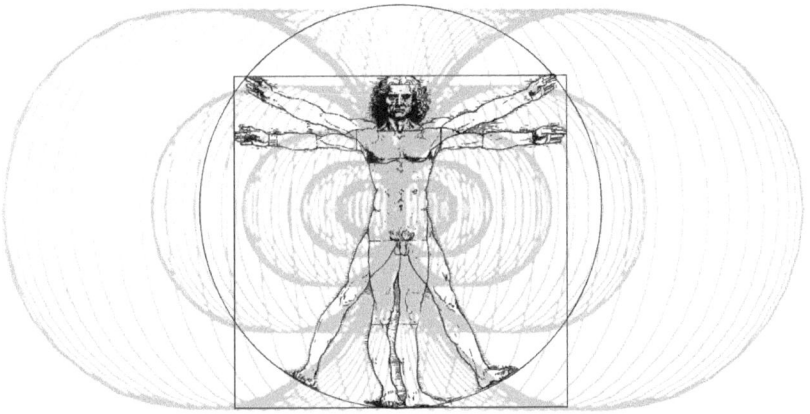

If we look with other eyes, and in another way at the world however, we see delightful and reassuring simplicity.

If we look at the world and observe fundamental pattern, we find, if we look innocently enough, and simply enough, and deeply enough - that there is only one, single, simple organizing principle that is the seed inside all things, large and small, from atom to galaxy. A seed pattern that under different circumstances and with different influences may generate a stone or a plant or an animal, or a planet - or a person.

A seed pattern that is fundamental to everything, that is shared universally throughout creation, that announces and reveals the true brother-sisterhood of everything around us, and assures us of our place in the family of things.

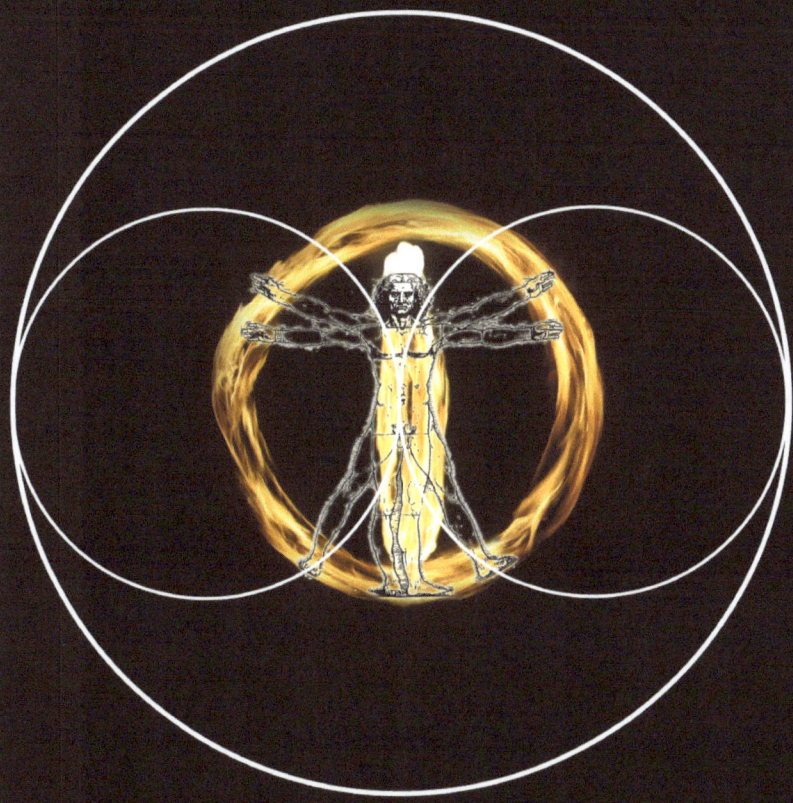

Let us consider a simple magnet.

The magnet has physical substance - is visible, is tangible, is touchable. At each end it has an equal but opposite magnetic charge or polarity - the north and south magnetic poles.

Between these complementary, balanced, opposite polarities a magnetic field arises, connecting the north and south poles with lines of force - the lines of magnetic flux - filling the space around the physical object with invisible energy.

Small, magnetically sensitive particles and objects may be drawn into and held by this invisible field of energy, revealing its' shape by the visible pattern that they form.

The shape of this invisible energy field, created by the presence of a pair of opposite polarities, is called a "toroid".

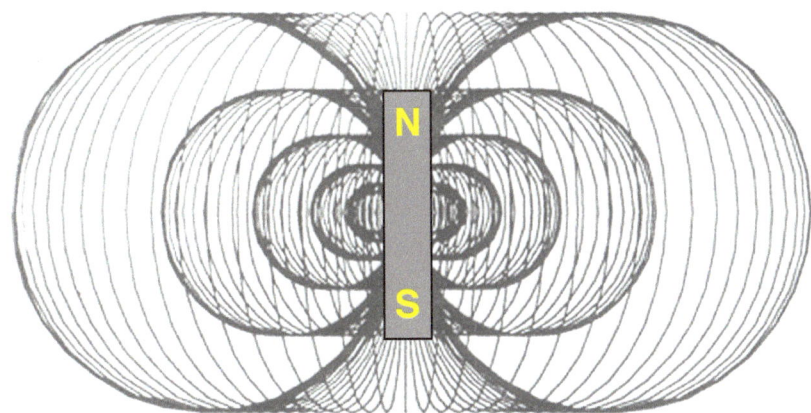

A dramatic and awe-inspiring example of a dynamic, powerful toroidal energy is the tornado.

In a tornado, the complementary opposite polarities are not magnetic, but are polarities of temperature and pressure. As with the magnet, these polarities create an invisible toroidal field of energy, which in this case moves not magnetically sensitive particles, but instead moves the substance of air creating powerful winds.

At the center of this invisible energy field, the forces may be strong enough to support a column of physical substance.

From the very small to the very large, this principle applies - a pair of complementary opposites create an invisible field of energy between them, which in it's central core may be dense enough and strong enough to support physical substance.

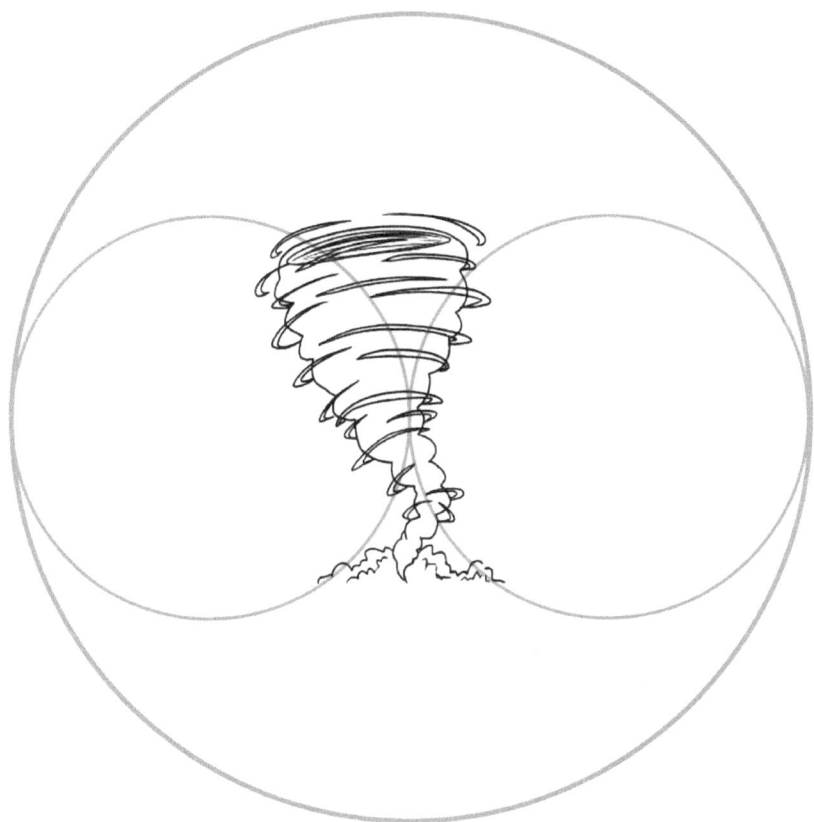

Learning about your Light Body

There are many names for the invisible energy field surrounding a human being, as well as different names for the concentric layers which may be experienced within it.

We shall take a very simple approach here - because in simplicity can truth be most easily appreciated.

The dense, central core of our light body is strong enough, like the tornado, to support physical structure - our physical body.

Permeating this and extending an inch or so beyond our physical edge, is a thermal and electromagnetic field or body which we can perceive when we bring our hands close together - we experience an "almost touching" before we actually make skin contact. This part of the light body is held to hold the blue print for our physical form.

Beyond this, we are surrounded by what we might consider our "personal emotional space". This space extends to approximately arms length all around us. If somebody comes this close to us, we definitely feel them to be "in our space" - either welcome or unwelcome. This part of the light body is held to contain our emotions.

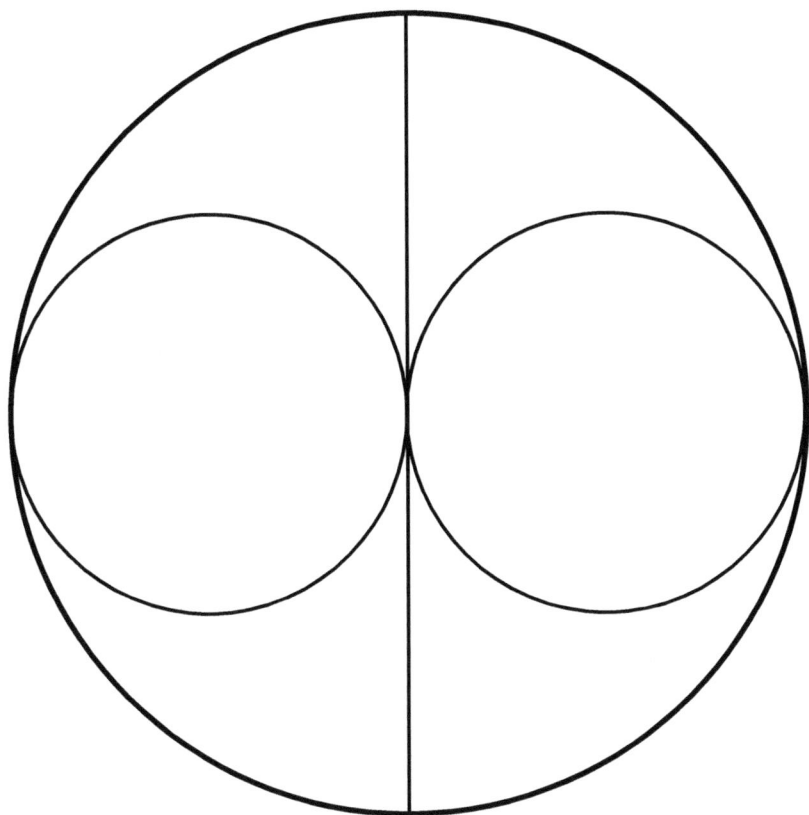

The next edge of ourselves that we can be easily aware of, if we pay attention to it, defines the space inside which most of our thoughts and thinking occur. It is typically a space surrounding us and extending about six feet in every direction. We may notice that most of our attention is contained or held by objects within that area, and we notice that we are naturally and easily able to communicate with people within that space, almost as though we were sharing thoughts and ideas intimately and wordlessly, as when sitting together around the kitchen table.

To communicate with another person at a distance beyond about six feet, we need to be more careful of words and concepts, as the natural intimacy of wordless meaning can be easily lost and communication requires more focussed attention and care to be sure that we are clearly understood and understanding.

Experiment for yourself with these three layers of your invisible energy field or light body, the very dense and close almost-physical layer, the personal emotional space, and the space of thought, attention and communication.

Notice that they are as much a part of yourself and of your experience of yourself in the world as is your physical body.

If we wish to improve and maintain the health and vigor of our physical body, we attend to it's physical needs - of appropriate shelter, clothing and food, of exercise, recreation and rest.

Equally, if we wish to improve and maintain the health and vitality of our light body, it is appropriate to give it the attention and care that it may need at it's more subtle level of vibrational harmony.

The quality of vibrational energy that we hold in our light body is perhaps the most defining factor in how we feel, moment by moment, and in how we experience the world around us.

It is the content and quality of thoughts and feelings and the vibrational tones of attitude in the light body, that polarize us like magnets to make the connections - with other people, events and circumstances - that create our personal experience of reality.

Here, in the fluid, ever moving tide of vibrational energy invisibly surrounding us, can we truly choose and create patterns of personal truth and beauty, and polarize them into existence for ourself through the laws of magnetic attraction.

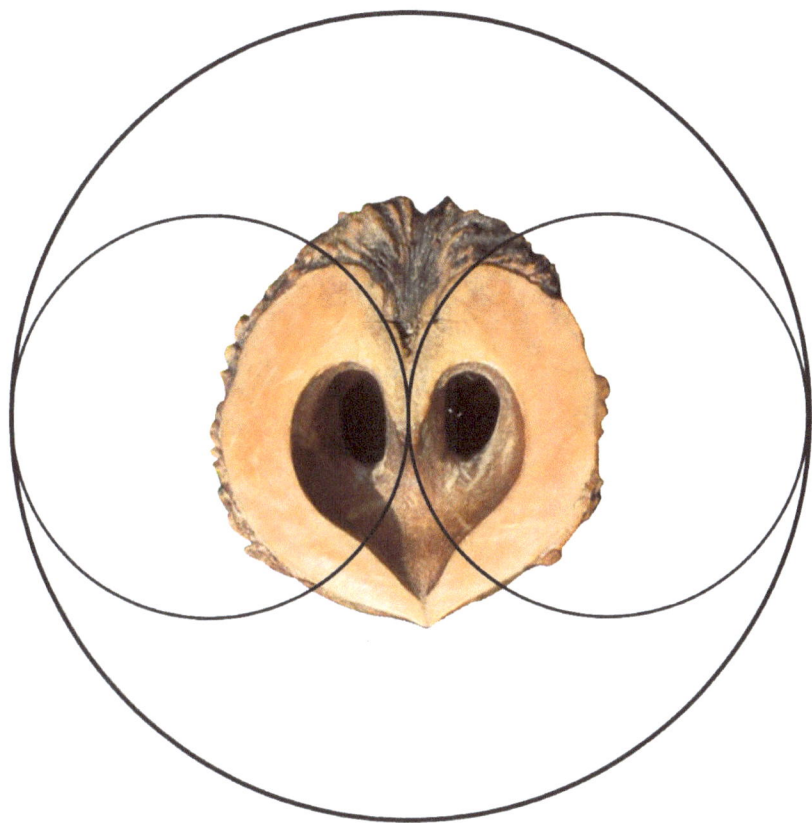

Consciousness is Vibration.

All consciousness is vibration - rhythm, harmony and tone - and all things vibrate.

Vibrations connect and communicate as waves moving between things through time and space, and become the defining tones and qualities of things when they orbit around and around centers of consciousness.

There is an infinite variety of possible vibrations, changing in large and small ways with variation of frequency, wavelength, wave-shape and the harmonic relationship between two or more vibrations, either the same or different.

Our physical sensations, our instincts and feelings, our thoughts and inspirations, are all vibrations of different kinds.

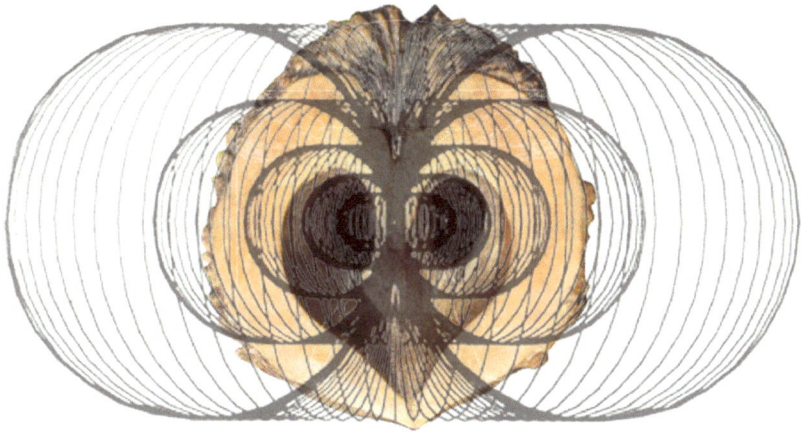

By measuring the electrical rhythm of our hearts and of our brains as thoughts and feelings change, we can see that each thought and feeling has a unique vibrational signature, and that as waves of sound and pressure and electro-magnetism, these vibrations are held and transmitted within our physical body, and within our light body surrounding us, and are transmitted far beyond us into our surrounding environment to the edge of our imagination - and beyond.

We can consider our light body to be our personal invisible energetic environment, filled with the vibrations that we create, attract and resonate with, moment by moment, patterning our inner and outer world in the same way that the ocean waves create patterns in the sand on the beach.

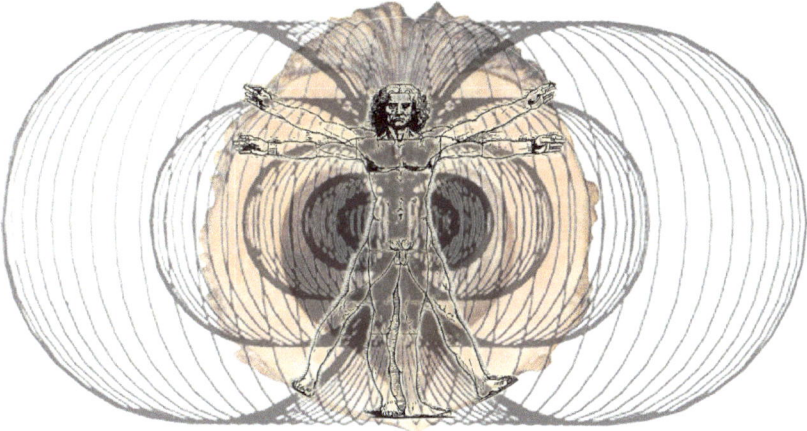

When we change the quality of vibration in the light body, we change the personal micro-environment in which we live.

Depending on the vibrations that we fill it with, the vibrations of thoughts and feelings, we may make it pleasant or unpleasant for ourself.

When we change the quality of vibration in the light body, we change the waves of magnetic polarity that attract or repel different people, events and circumstances in our life.

As we become aware of the quality and vibrational tone of our invisible, personal energetic space, we notice the inner and outer effects that it has.

As we learn to influence, manage and control those vibrations, we discover a most powerful way to choose and direct our life experiences, and to become the authors of our own happiness.

The Vibrations of Quality and Content

We can easily tell, when spoken communication is occurring, not only the specific meaning - assuming that we understand the words and language used - but also the feeling and attitude conveyed by the tone and quality of voice. The vibrations of the voice carry both content of thought and quality of feeling.

We may observe that the response elicited is often much more defined by the quality and tone of expressed feeling than by the actual language content itself.

This is true not only in individual conversation but also in the general law of attraction that so powerfully underwrites our life - we attract those things that we give our attention to, in the same resonant tone as that in which our attention is given.

Sad thoughts about a something will attract a sad experience of the something, happy thoughts about the same something will attract a happy experience of that same thing.

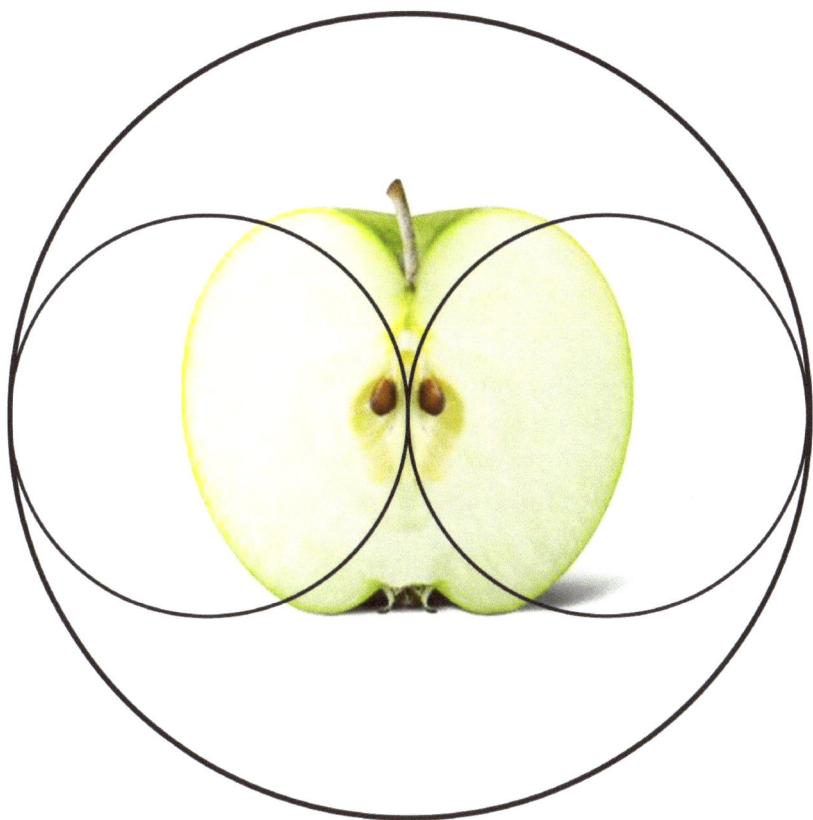

Circumstances Arise to Match our Mood

Human beings are mostly motivated towards happiness.

We pursue specific things in our life only to the extent that we expect or believe that having or experiencing those things will make us happy, from the outside in.

Happiness, like every other emotion, has its own vibrational tone, that we can generate and fill our light bodies with, by conscious choice and practice, from the inside out.

Like the ever changing patterns on the beach created by the waves of ocean, circumstances - like sand - conform to the quality and tone of the waves of emotion that we generate and hold in the space around us.

Happy feelings if consistently maintained, create happy patterns in the sand and happy events and circumstances on the beach of our life's experience.

When beginning to manage and control our vibrational energetic space, we place quality of feeling first and foremost, above content and detail of circumstance.

In this way can we begin to free ourselves from a sense of being the victim of the external, and begin to recreate our circumstances and life experiences from the inside out, through controlling the quality and tone of thought and feeling.

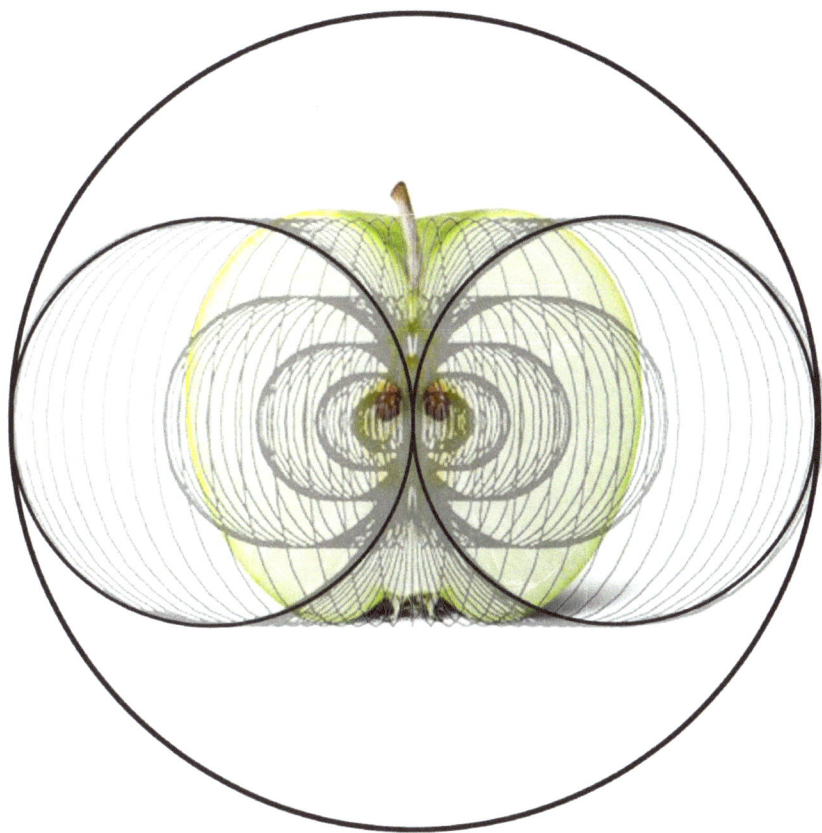

Vibrations of the Heart ~ Emanations of the Soul

At the center of our body, at the center of our seven-fold energy system, at the center of our life, is the Heart.

The heart is the primary generator of vibration, and therefore of consciousness, within our body. The strongest generator of electromagnetism in our energy field and the source of the pulse pressure wave that circulates blood and nourishment to every cell.

We might choose to consider that the vibrations of the heart are the pure and direct emanation of the consciousness of our soul into the physical dimension of our life.

When we allow the rhythm of the heart it's primary role, and allow all other vibration and consciousness within and around ourself to follow it's lead - allowing heart to govern breath, feeling and thought, we naturally enter into a state known as cardiac coherence - a state of heart centered oneness in joyous harmony with all of ourself and all of everything, our own naturally arising state of Grace.

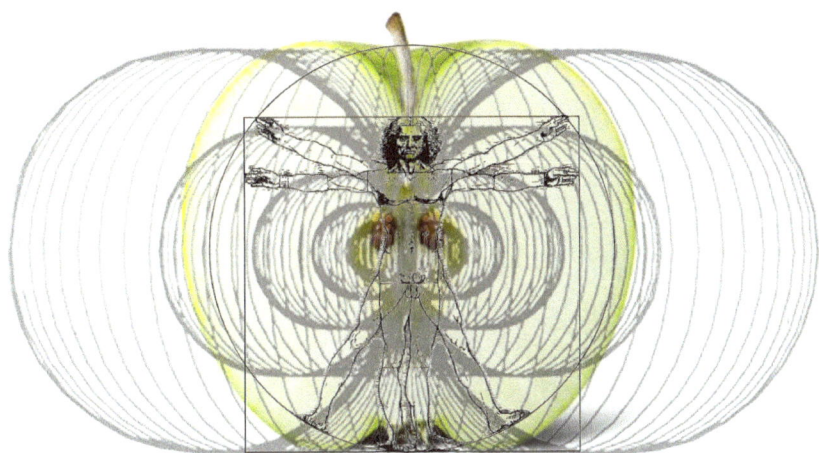

Grace is our most natural state.

It is the state from which we arise, and the state to which we return.

Along the way between, we learn through cycles of self-expression & self-reflection how to align the Small Will of the self with the Great Will of the soul, embracing and befriending the ego in the service of our higher mind until our social order becomes an expression of our divine nature.

When we allow our heart to freely express it's natural vibrations of grace, and to align ourself with that entirely, a cascade of vibrations in golden ratio proportion emanate throughout the light body, creating states experienced as those of simple joy and wonder, of happiness, and of being in the flow of our life.

When we allow discordant vibrations to overlay and mask those of heart's grace, we experience progressive degrees of fear and limitation within our patterns of thought and feeling, and in our experience of life's circumstances.

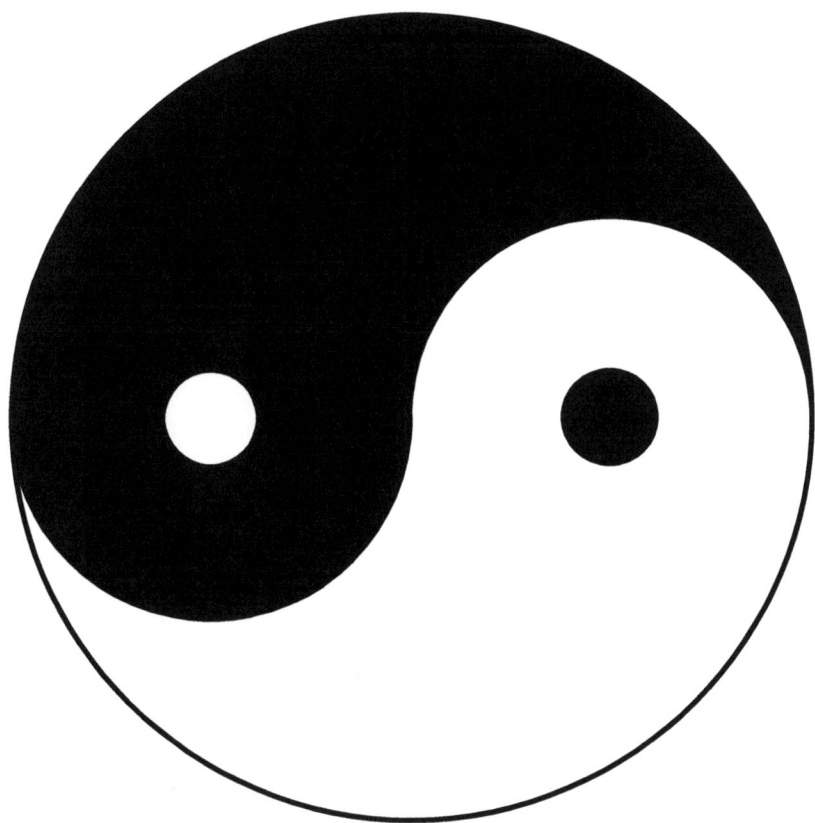

Cultivating the Light Body - a Practice for Your Life

Because the heart naturally fills the light body with grace - when free to express itself unencumbered by shrouds and clouds of fear and false belief -we need only allow the heart to become the conductor of the orchestra of our consciousness to return to our natural grace state.

For many of us the greatest difficulty in allowing this state to arise is the insistence of the logical mind to hold the role of executive director of life's affairs.

The vibrations emanating from a controlling state of mind are typically somewhat limited, fearful and distorted when compared to the heart's grace and wisdom.

When allowed to dictate and control the primary tone of vibrations in the light body, our life is limited by the limits of our mind and imagination.

Our logical mind however, is an organ of our psyche, an integral part of our human consciousness, as necessary and desirable to our life and our health as are our lungs and our liver.

A great and central key to restoring our natural state of grace is to switch the attitude and posture of our logical mind from one of executive control to one of simple, compassionate witness.

Practice #1

Assume a natural, resting posture, sitting or standing, spine erect. Allow your "inner athlete" to bring your physical body into an athletic, resting tone and posture throughout. Release all control of your breath, and begin to watch as your body breaths by itself.

Begin to smile at yourself - allow the smile to deepen and warm - allow the smile to smile not only on your face, but also on the soles of your feet, the palms of your hands, the top of your head.

When all of you is smiling, direct the warmth and love of the smile towards the center of your chest - send the loving warmth of your smile all the way to the center of your heart.

Continue to smile at your heart until you can feel the love warming, brightening and filling the heart, as a strong sensation.

Feel ever more strongly the love arriving in your heart. Feel the heart receiving all of your love.

And then allow yourself to experience yourself AS the heart receiving the love.

Allow the mind to become a simple and compassionate witness of the heart, and of that which arises from the heart.

Allow the sensations of the body to be witness to the vibrations and consciousness arising from the heart.

Allow body and mind, sensation and thought, to witness as you, the heart, from yourself, from your heart, from the center of your being in the center of your chest, fill the whole of your physical body and the whole of your invisible personal energetic space - your light body - with the irrepressible vibrations of your souls' natural grace.

Compassionately witnessing as joy and peace and simple happiness arise, within and without. And let the heart guide the breath as it connects you to all creation.

Affirm that this is your natural state in which to live in the world.

Practice #2

First bring yourself to the heart centered state of practice #1, allowing the mind to relax into a posture of pleasant and compassionate witness, and the heart to be the vibrational source of intelligence, guiding breath, and guiding posture, filling the body and the light body with its natural state of grace.

Allow yourself to become aware of your primary axis of alignment, the alignment between the top of your head and the root of the pelvis, the central channel of your invisible toroidal energy field.

An alignment passing centrally through the heart - a column of light and radiance - a single, simple balanced cord of subtle vibration - perfectly stable, like the spindle at the center of a gyroscope - like the gently vibrating string of a musical instrument.

And become aware of the extended connection of this vibrant core energy to the center of the planet, the magnetic connection between your heart and the center of the world... between your heart and the center of the world heart.

And then become aware of the vibrant connection from the heart upwards through the crown of your head to the source point of your heaven self in the realms above.

Feel the strength and clarity and brightness of that connection, a stable, gyroscopic alignment connecting you to heaven and earth, heart centered, in natural grace.

With this central channel stable and bright, allow your awareness to extend outward in every direction to become fully aware of the radiant personal space surrounding you, the whole of your light body, its depth and volume, and the clear, bright edges where it meets the surrounding world.

Maintaining your central awareness of yourself as your heart, and using the mind and the sensations of your body only as witness and guide, allow yourself to explore and perceive any patterns of tension or unresolved trauma, displacement or disintegration, held or present within your body or light body.

Using mind and body as witness and guide, allow the heart's radiance and core intelligence to simply reconnect and renew all and every part of yourself that you find in disharmony, effortlessly renewing the patterns on the sand with natural grace.

Allowing the heart's compassion and intelligence to surround, resolve and integrate all the patterns of energetic disharmony within your body and the radiant space surrounding you.

Once you feel a full return to stable, heart-defined grace throughout yourself, allow your mind's witness to return to heart breath, and affirm that this is your natural state in which to live in the world.

Practice #3

Following practices 1 & 2, rest ever more deeply into your experience of self as heart-self, until your primary awareness of self and environment is peacefully and steadily located in, and arising from, the center of your chest - the center of your heart.

Gently, gradually, and completely, receive and witness the heart's radiance projecting as a loving wave of energy and intelligence throughout every part of your body, and out beyond your body where it forms and fills your personal space around you - cleansing and renewing every part of you, and the edges of you where you meet the world.

Once you are feeling fully peaceful, stable and centered in your heart, bring into conscious awareness any current issue, concern, person or situation that is causing you distress or disharmony.

As you bring the issue to mind, allow yourself to experience it in a globally integrated manner, observing simultaneously the thought, the feeling, the attitude, the sensation, and the instinctual response or reaction.

Allow yourself to witness the energy pattern as a wave of consciousness, a wave that in some small or large way has become incoherent, out of tune or somehow lacking in balance.

Maintaining an attitude of simple compassionate witness, allow your mind and body to guide the heart's awareness, and with it the bright blessing of healing and renewal that it brings... into and around the stressful patterns that you perceive.

Gratefully witness a full and complete restoration of peace, ease and vitality into every part of your awareness, until you find a place of heart centered grace in the presence of the issue of your original concern. Stay in the cycle of witness and heart blessing until you feel peace and creative inspiration arise... and then gently release your issue from thought and feeling for now.

Having done this, next extend your awareness throughout the space inside yourself, and throughout the space around you, including the edge of your light body, and become aware of any threads or cords, or pathways of energy, thought or feeling, connecting you to other people, to other places or events, past present or future.

Notice whether these pathways are open or closed, active or passive, peaceful or stressful - notice if they are contemporary and appropriate to yourself as you are now.

As before, use your mind and global awareness to direct the heart's radiant intelligence to those pathways of connection that feel ill at ease or inappropriate in any way.

Witness the return to a natural state of grace that occurs as the heart renews, in simple truth and beauty, the nature and quality of the connections between you and your world, bringing each one into a state of peace, health, and balance.

Once you feel yourself, and your connective relationships, renewed in a natural state of grace, allow yourself to return to a simple witness of your breath, its depth and rhythm, feeling the full wave of your breath throughout the length of your spine.

Allow yourself to integrate this heart centered awareness of self as normal, as natural, and as your place in which to be as you move in the world.

Extending Your Light Body Awareness to other people and to everything in your environment...

All things that have a stable form have their own light body. Each person, animal, bird and insect, every plant and tree - every place and every planet.

By extending the subtle awareness that we develop of our own light body, we can perceive and relate to the resonance and consciousness within those things around us.

At this level of awareness, we can develop a resonance and rapport much deeper and richer than through the use of words and language alone, and find within the exchange a deep understanding and compassion for the other - a sense of the inner spirit and true nature much deeper than that defined either by our social masks or intellectual judgments.

We typically experience this subliminal rapport with our close friends and family, with companion animals, and with places that are special to us.

Cultivating your light body thus results in both an increase in health, vitality and clarity in yourself, as well as an increased capacity to perceive, relate to, and creatively influence everything around you.

Practicing Extended Light Body Awareness.

Once you feel confident and stable in a heart centered space with a bright, healthy light body, begin to consciously connect from your own heart to the heart of others. This will feel natural with friends and family, and perhaps when first beginning somewhat strange and unfamiliar with others.

We are mostly used to meeting other people with our minds when in conversation and in our feelings and sensations when sharing activities together. The global awareness arising from meeting in the heart however, naturally includes thoughts and feelings, sensations and instinct, but also includes the subliminal resonances of soul and spirit.

When we connect heart to heart, we exchange and experience, in a peaceful present way, something of the totality of each of us, and if the tone and quality of connection is one of compassion, we open creative potential far greater than that which arises if we connect with each other in a more limited way with thought alone.

By maintaining heart connection and peaceful compassion in our exchanges, we begin to create circumstances and opportunities otherwise unimagined.

Healing and the Light Body

Researchers studying the balance and range of waves in the electrical patterns around the brain, identified a particular state of coherence and symmetry which appeared during meditation, yoga, dowsing and spiritual healing.

When studying the patterns in healers and those who came to them, it was observed that the healer first entered what we might term a Grace state, following which their patient's resonant patterns began to change, as if by entrainment or sympathetic resonance, towards the same state of Grace.

The return of coherent symmetry in the patient's electrical resonance was usually associated with some degree of help and benefit in the condition of original concern.

This understanding offers us all enormous potential to benefit those around us, friends family and community, in a simple and non-intrusive way - by holding a Grace state in our light body we naturally enhance the tone of any interaction, situation or circumstance - and when we allow or offer another person to resonate sympathetically, we can share and multiply grace just like exchanging a smile.

We do this naturally with those very close and intimate, and there are many modalities of energetic healing becoming increasingly popular and common as models for this most natural and simple form of human caring.

Regardless of the outer form of a healing technique, the sharing of a coherent state of resonance between those involved is universal.

When holding a bright, clear, coherent and graceful resonance for healing to occur, it seems wisest and best during the process to maintain the logical mind in a poise of compassionate witness - a benevolent unconditional observer - allowing for the presence of discord to be witnessed but without oneself becoming engaged or distracted by it.

If we find our self unable to hold a fully compassionate witness during a healing session, it is best to pause and allow one's own grace to return before proceeding.

When we have completed and closed a healing exchange, it is good to tune in to our self and ensure that our own light body is well maintained in its natural state of grace, and if any discord has arisen to give whatever time and attention is necessary to restore peaceful resonance there.

Sharing the Love.

When our light body is bright, we brighten the tone and atmosphere around us, and when we share our heart resonance we create pathways for creative exchange between our self and whatever we give our attention to.

This interactive spreading of grace and vitality through the waves of resonance arising from loving attention, has been shown to occur not only between individual people, but also between people, plants and animals, as well as between our human intelligence and the atmosphere and intelligence of landscape and place.

People with "green fingers" are often those who most naturally resonate in a sympathetic way with the wave forms and frequencies within and around the plants that they tend, creating a mutually beneficial exchange of life energy and nourishing vitality.

Those living or working closely with animals are equally familiar with the close exchange of communication that occurs when we are in resonance with them, each species having its own slightly unique and particular pattern of tone and intelligence that defines it as itself.

Spreading the Love.

Numerous studies around the world have shown beneficial changes in social parameters, crime statistics and sometimes political crises following a period of focused healing attention being given to the local Spirit of Place, or offered into the Spirit of the Community concerned.

This can be done individually, and gathers a multiplying effect when shared collectively with a group.

A very simple and proven technique when healing of place is required, is to identify the local "geomantic centre" - perhaps the market cross, village green or some defining central point of community orientation in a town - or perhaps a point of special atmosphere and aesthetic in the landscape - and to direct attention there as a point of connection to the surrounding web.

Healing energy can be exchanged with the resonance and intelligence of landscape in exactly the same way that it is exchanged between people - first brightening and balancing our own light body, and then sharing the waves of naturally arising grace through our unconditionally loving attention - either when we are physically present, or when offering the same quality of attention at a distance through thought and imagination.

Using this simple technique of unconditional loving attention, we can direct beneficial creative life force to anything that we can conceive of in our minds.

We can nurture and enhance the spirit of our family, of our enterprise - the spirit of our community and our culture - all things come to life more fully with our love.

Try it and see...

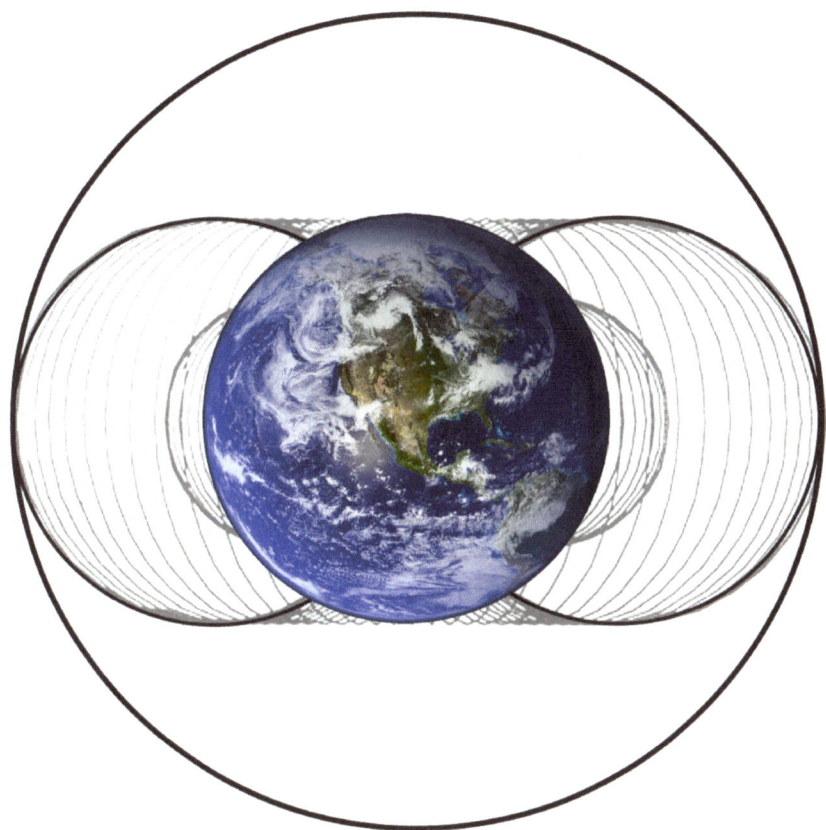

Dr. Patrick MacManaway

Patrick MacManaway learned about consciousness and metaphysics at his parent's kitchen table, from the many extraordinary and talented people who visited, taught and studied at their healing, teaching and natural therapies center in rural Scotland.

A holistic practitioner, consultant and educator, Patrick holds a degree in Medicine from Edinburgh University, is past President of the British Society of Dowsers and a founding member of Circles for Peace.

Through the practices of teaching students and parenting his daughter Alya, Patrick seeks to share key principles in a simple, inviting and empowering fashion.

This handbook is one of a series presenting the essential foundational elements inside the rich traditions of spirituality and philosophy that our new age has inherited.

You can find out about Patrick's work on his website
www.PatrickMacManaway.com

The Simply Good Company

Products for Whole-Hearted Living

You can find a full range of Patrick's books
and CDs, and browse through our
catalogue of inspirational offerings

Visit us online
www.SimplyGoodCo.com

To educate and inspire

Celebrating Grace in the Landscape...

www.CirclesforPeace.org

www.ingramcontent.com/pod-product-compliance
Lightning Source LLC
LaVergne TN
LVHW010031070426
835508LV00005B/295